Citizenship and PSHE
Book 2

Contents

Deena Haydon
Pat King
Christine Moorcroft

Different feelings

 How does Sam feel in these pictures?

 1. Copy and complete the table.

Picture	How Sam feels	How I can tell
a		
b		
c		

Word bank

afraid	calm	frightened	relaxed
angry	cross	happy	sad
bad-tempered	excited	joyful	unhappy

2. With a partner, think of four words that describe feeling good and four words that describe feeling bad.

Feeling good	Feeling bad

Make a display of everybody's words.

3. In pairs, take turns to talk about a time when you felt really good.

What made you feel like that?

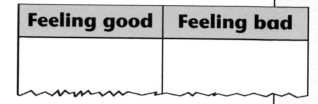

I felt really good when Mr Peters told me how pleased he was with my work.

What did you do? What happened next?

People show their feelings in different ways.

When I'm upset, I go very quiet.

When I'm happy, I sing!

4. What might you do if you felt:

happy?   upset?   angry?
excited?   scared?   shy?

How do people show their feelings?

What makes me feel this way?

Things that happen around us can affect our feelings.

 1. Talk to a partner about how Greg feels in each picture.

 2. What might have happened before Greg arrived at school? Copy and complete the table.

Day	How Greg felt	What might have happened
Monday		
Tuesday		
Wednesday		

 3. Draw and write what might happen next on Monday, Tuesday and Wednesday.

Think about:
– what Greg might do
– what his friends might do.

Sometimes there seems to be no reason for our feelings.

ⓐ Everyone suddenly burst out singing;
And I was filled with such delight
As prisoned birds must find in freedom
Winging wildly across the white
Orchards and dark green fields; on – on – and out of sight.

From *Everyone Sang* by Siegfried Sassoon

ⓑ

I'm sad in my tummy
And I don't know why.
I don't feel like playing
I only want to cry.

From *Sad* by Michelle Magorian

4. What feelings do the two poems describe?
How can you tell?

Copy and complete the table.

Poem	Feeling	How I can tell
a		
b		

5. Describe someone who feels angry but does not know why.
What might he or she do?

You could make up a poem about someone who feels angry.

Points of view

A school to be closed

Small Lane school in Little Village is a hundred-year-old building with a tiny playground. Along one side of the playground is a narrow garden, which all the children and the headteacher look after. The school is surrounded by fields. In one of the fields is a pond in which there are frogs, many kinds of pond insects and even smooth newts. At the end of the summer term, Small Lane school is going to be closed because it has only fourteen pupils aged from four to nine.

The children will go to Large Street school in Big Village, five miles away. Large Street school has ninety-six pupils aged from four to eleven. It is a big modern building and it has a much bigger playground. The playground has shady trees, benches and tables and it has markings for games like hopscotch and giant snakes and ladders.

 What might the children of the two schools think about the changes?

 1. With a partner, list anything that might worry the children.

Copy and complete the table.

Small Lane children	Large Street children

Think about travel, getting used to a new building, things left behind, sharing with new children and making new friends.

2. Imagine you are a pupil at either Small Lane or Large Street school.

 Write a letter to your teacher about your worries.

People have different ideas about what time eight-year-olds should go to bed on weekdays.

They should be in bed by eight o'clock.

Nine o'clock is early enough.

We should go to bed when we feel tired.

What do you think?

3. With a partner, discuss the time at which you think eight-year-olds should go to bed.

Give your reasons.

4. With your partner, write an information leaflet for eight-year-olds about sensible bedtimes.

Think about:
- the things children have to do in the evening
- the things they want to do
- the time they have to get up in the morning.

Do they need to go to bed at the same time every night?

1. Talk to a partner about what Kate must do to make sure she can look after her rabbit.

Think about finding information, remembering things like feeding and cleaning, and people who can help.

2. Write a letter to Kate, to:

- give her encouragement
- suggest what she needs to find out
- give her ideas about **remembering** to care for her rabbit.

Jason is going to stay at his friend Mark's house.
He is looking forward to it but he has a few concerns.

I don't know where the bathroom is.

I don't know what to call Mark's parents.

I might not like the meals.

I don't know Mark's dad. He looks strict.

I won't know where to put my things.

I might not get on with his sister.

3. Talk to a partner about Jason's concerns.
What other concerns might he have?

4. What advice would you give Jason?
Write your suggestions in a table.

Jason's concern	Your advice
I don't know where the bathroom is.	Ask Mark to show you around when you get there.

Think about the information Jason needs, how he can find it and what he could do or say.

5. How can Mark help Jason to feel at home?

What can be helpful when things seem difficult?

What is an 'issue'?

Issues are problems that need to be solved. They might be about people, places, events, food, lifestyles ... .

 1. Are you worried about any issues like these?
List some issues that are important to you.

Copy and complete the table.

Issues at home	Issues in school	Issues in our community	Issues in the world

Sometimes people do not agree about what causes a problem, or how it could be solved.

Great, now we won't have to go into the city to watch a film.

Raj

LOCAL NEWS:
Plans to build new cinema.

NOW SHOWING...
SPACE WARS 2

Kate

Yes, but the social club for senior citizens is going to be knocked down to make room for the cinema.

citizenship

2. In a group, think about the different views of Raj and Kate.
Do you think the cinema should be built?
What other information would help you to make your decision?
Record your ideas in a table.

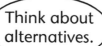
Think about alternatives.

Think about consequences.

Reasons for building a cinema	Reasons against building a cinema	What we need more information about	Alternatives

Use these ideas to develop a short play that includes the different points of view. What is your solution?

3. When you are discussing an issue, what do you need to do before you can make up your own mind?

Think about:
– 'fact' finding
– listening to others
– using more than one source of information
– different views and opinions.

4. Where could you obtain information to help you discuss issues and make decisions?

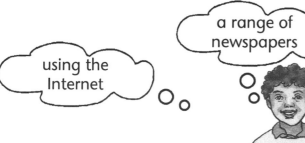

a range of newspapers

interviewing an expert

using the Internet

Hear both sides of the argument
I think   I think

5. Draw a poster to remind people about important decision-making skills.

Doing the right thing

 1. How are these children behaving?

Think of words to describe their behaviour.

Word bank

caring
considerate
helpful
polite
thoughtful

 2. What encourages people to behave in responsible ways?

It feels good to be kind to someone.

 I try to share because I know what it feels like to be left out.

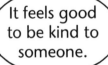

I want people to like me.

I prefer my mum to be smiling. I don't like it when she looks upset.

In our class we get a certificate for being helpful.

3. Find out what
'antisocial' means.
Draw a picture of someone
whose behaviour is
antisocial.
What words could be
used to describe
antisocial behaviour?

Word bank	
destructive	rude
frightening	threatening
harmful	uncaring
hurtful	

4. How do you think each of the five people in the picture feels
about what has happened?
Do you think the children care or are upset?
If they care, what could they do?
If they do not care, what might be their reasons?

5. Everyone can learn to change
their behaviour.

What do you think should
happen to people who behave
in antisocial ways?

Should all
antisocial behaviour be
treated in the
same way?

How can you behave in responsible ways?

Making decisions

1. Make a list of all the choices Marcus and Ryan could make – their 'options'.

What would influence their decisions?
What might the consequences of each choice be?
Copy and complete the table.

Think about:
– how they feel
– how others might feel
– the consequences.

Option	Influences	Consequences
Tell an adult	Not wanting to get into trouble An adult can help make a decision	
Keep the watch	Excitement	

What about the person who lost the watch?

If they don't take it, someone else will.

They'll get found out and then they'll be in trouble.

2. What choice do you think they should make?

Choices usually affect more than one person – you and other people.

3. What do we need to think about when we make choices?

4. Discuss with a partner what options Becky has. What would you say and do if you were Becky?

5. Make a list of words describing how Becky and her mum might feel:
a. if Becky tidies her room
b. if Becky persuades her mum to let her go out with her friends.

Word bank

annoyed	pleased
disappointed	proud
grateful	relaxed
happy	relieved
hurt	upset
offended	

What do you need to think about when you make decisions?

Consequences

 1. What could happen to the children in the pictures?
Choose one of the actions.
Draw a set of pictures showing what people say and think
before and after the event.
Begin by completing this example.

Before

After

Any choice has a consequence.

2. Make a list of the kinds of things that might happen as the result of a choice you make.
Make a table.

Think about:
– feelings
– actions
– self
– others.

Positive consequences	Negative consequences
receiving a reward	being told off
helping others	harming others
feeling good	feeling ashamed

3. Who is responsible for the consequences of an action, or for behaviour?

Lisa   Tom   Dan   Abdul   Sarah   Mike   May

4. What is happening in the picture? What are the options for each child?

Record the options in a table.

Child	Options
Lisa Dan Abdul Sarah	could 1. 2. 3.

5. Who do you think is responsible for doing something about this bullying behaviour?
Is it the bullies?
Is it the person being bullied?
Is it anyone who knows about the bullying?
Is it adults, children or both?

Give reasons for your answers.

Who is responsible for your behaviour and actions?

Making difficult decisions

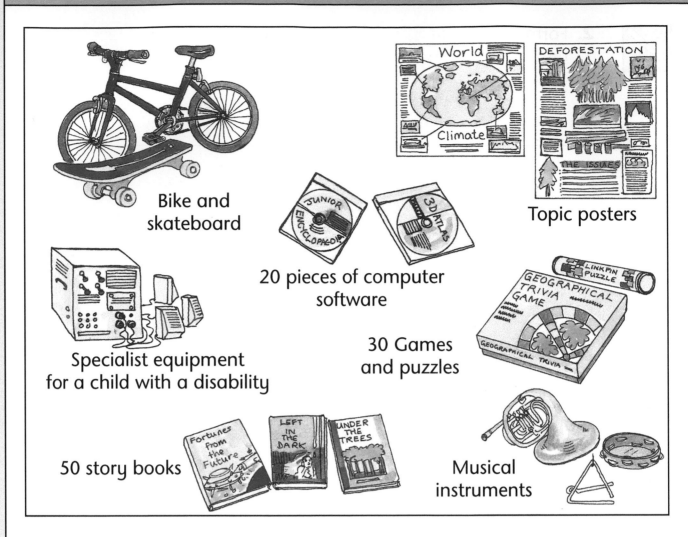

Bike and skateboard

Topic posters

20 pieces of computer software

Specialist equipment for a child with a disability

30 Games and puzzles

50 story books

Musical instruments

A class of eight- and nine-year-olds has been given money to spend on a set of resources. They can only afford one set.

1. Which set of resources do you think they should buy?

Record your reasons

> I think the class should buy
> _____ because _____
> _____ .

Think about:
– who can use them
– when they can be used
– whether they are needed
– whether they are a luxury.

Discuss your reasons with a partner.
Do you agree with each other?

2. Form a group of people who have all made the same choice. In your group, make a list of all the reasons for buying your chosen set of resources.

Group A

Choice – story books

Reasons
– everyone can use them

Group B

Choice – computer software

Reasons
– help us to learn ICT skills

3. Listen to the reasons of each group.
Take a class vote on which choice to make.
Can you all agree on one set of resources?
What did you think about when making your decision?

I think we should choose something that will be useful for everyone.

I think we should choose something that can be used all the time, not just in the summer.

I think we should spend the money on something we don't already have.

I think we should buy something that will help someone who needs extra support.

What needs to be considered when resources are allocated?

Taking part

Class 6 has a decision to make.

 1. How do you think the class could make this decision?

The children of class 6 take a vote and record the options.

Farm	Museum	Theme Park	Swimming pool
IIII	IIII	LHʹI	II

2. How many children wanted to go to the theme park?
How many children wanted to go somewhere else?
Because the Theme Park had the most votes, the class decided to go there.
Do you think this was fair?

3. When choices are made, some people do not get what they want.

How might they feel about this?

What could be done to help solve this problem?

Word bank

angry
disappointed
ignored
frustrated
left out
upset

4. Four children in class 6 did not vote.
At playtime, they told their friends that they would prefer to go to the museum.
  – What would you say to them if they were your friends?
  – Would their votes have made a difference?
  – Should the class have another vote?

5. What decisions do you think you should be asked to make as part of a group?

Copy and complete the table.

Group	Decisions
sports team	– position on team – team captain
class	

How can you make a difference in group decisions?

Growing and changing

a   b   c

d   e   f

1. Which people are older than you?
How can you tell they are older?
How are they different from you?

	Same or older	How can you tell?
a		
b		

You have grown and changed a lot since you were born.
You will change and grow more.

Discuss your answers with a partner.

2. How will you change between now and:
– age 12
– age 17?

Lifestyle

3. How has Rosie's grandad changed?

My grandad (on the right) when he was nine.

My grandad now. He is taller and fatter. His head is a bit bald. He has a beard and a moustache.

These objects are linked to growing up.

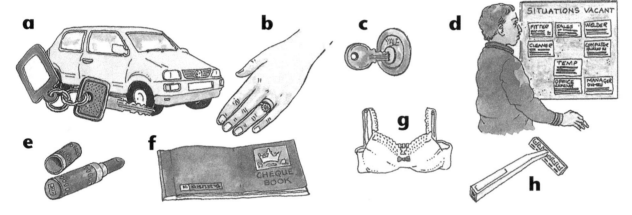

a **b** **c** **d**

e **f** **g**

h

SITUATIONS VACANT

CHEQUE BOOK

4. How old would someone be when they first use these things?

Copy and complete the table. Explain your answers.

5. Draw and describe other things that people use when they are grown up.

Object	Age	Reason
a		
b		

What is better about being:
– your age?
– grown up?

What do you look forward to about growing up?

New baby

These women are pregnant. Soon they will each have a baby.

a

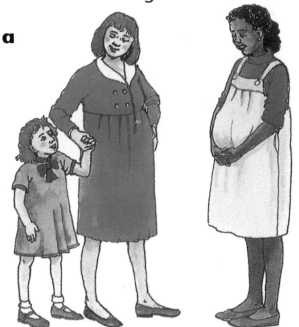

The inside story

b This picture shows the position of the baby. It will be born in a few days' time.

Before it is born, the baby does not need to eat or breathe. It gets all it needs from inside its mother's body. It grows bigger, wriggles and kicks.

1. How can you tell from picture **a** that the women are pregnant?

What do you notice about the baby in picture **b**?

Notice the position of the baby and which way up it is.

A baby grows from an egg. All animals grow from eggs.

2. Draw a hen's egg, life size.
Next to it draw a life-size frog's egg. Then draw a butterfly's egg. Finally, draw a human egg, the size of a pinpoint.

3. Find out about other animals' eggs. Which ones grow inside their mothers? Which hatch outside?

Animal	Eggs grow inside	Hatch outside

Before a woman's egg can grow into a baby it has to be joined by a sperm from a man.

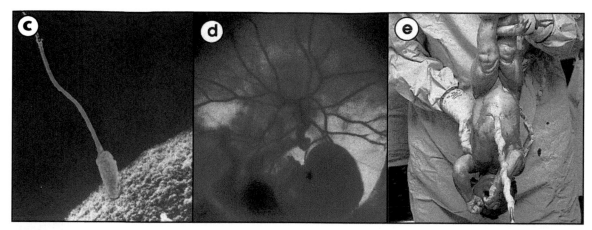

The sperm and egg join together.

The egg then grows into a baby.

About nine months later, the baby is born.

4. What changes can you see, from egg to baby?

What can a new-born baby do?
What can't it do?
What has to be done for it?

As babies grow, they can do more.

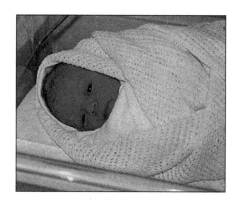

5. Find out when babies usually learn to do different things, such as walk, talk and feed themselves.

Age	What the baby can do
4 months	Eat solid food.
	Sit up.

6. Collect pictures of things that babies need.
Why do they need them?
Display what you have discovered.

How do people encourage babies to learn new things?

Leisure and work

This is how John and his family spent their time one Wednesday.

John's mother's day:

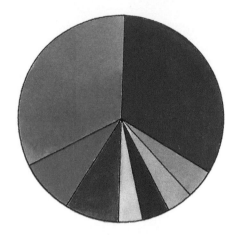

John's mother

8 hours at work
8 hours asleep
1 hour washing and dressing
1 hour travelling by car
1 hour watching TV
1 hour reading
2 hours cooking, cleaning and eating
2 hours with family

John

6 hours at school
10 hours asleep
$\frac{1}{2}$ hour walking to and from school
$\frac{1}{2}$ hour homework
$\frac{1}{2}$ hour washing and dressing
$\frac{1}{2}$ hour tidying up and washing up
1 hour computer games
1 hour football
$1\frac{1}{2}$ hours watching TV
$1\frac{1}{2}$ hours eating and relaxing
1 hour with family

John's father

8 hours at work
8 hours asleep
1 hour washing and dressing
1 hour travelling by train
1 hour cooking, cleaning and eating
1 hour with family
1 hour gardening
2 hours watching TV
1 hour reading

 1. Look at John's mother's pie chart. How did she spend most of her time?

 2. Make pie charts for John and his father. Use different colours to show what they did.

 3. How much time did each person spend on work and how much time on leisure? Make a table.

	John	Father
work		
leisure		

 4. Make a pie chart to show how you spent one weekday.

What is the difference between work and leisure?

5. Copy and complete the table.

Activity	Work or leisure?
digging	
writing	

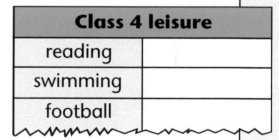
Add some activities of your own to the table.

6. What are your three favourite ways of enjoying yourself?

Class 4 leisure	
reading	
swimming	
football	

7. Make a tally chart and a graph to show what the children in your class do for leisure.

What is the most popular activity?
Which pastimes are energetic?
Which are relaxing?

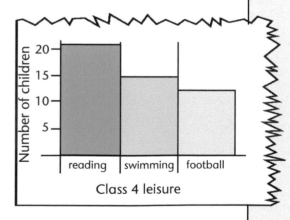

8. Make a list to show how you spent your time yesterday.

What energetic things did you do?
What relaxing things did you do?

Exercise

 In what ways is your body like a machine?

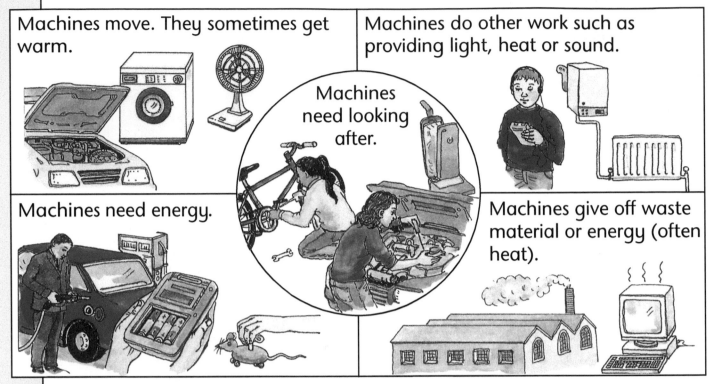

Machines move. They sometimes get warm.

Machines do other work such as providing light, heat or sound.

Machines need looking after.

Machines need energy.

Machines give off waste material or energy (often heat).

 1. Copy and complete this table.

What it does or needs	My body (✔ ✗)	A machine (✔ ✗)
moves		
gets warm		

Exercise is one way to look after your body.
Exercise helps your body to have:

stamina   strength   suppleness

 **2.** Find out what these three words mean.

3. Look at the photographs.
How do the activities help keep the people healthy and fit?

Do they give strength, stamina or suppleness (they may give all three)?

Exercise	Strength	Stamina	Suppleness
a			
b			

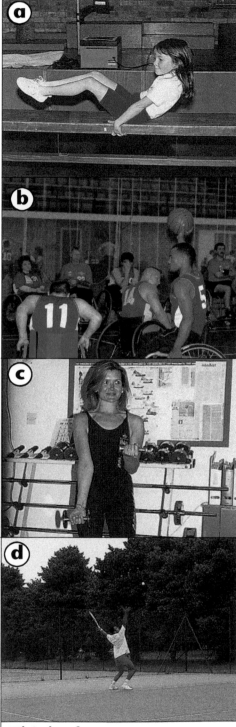

a

b

c

d

Think of some more exercises.

4. Draw an outline of your body, like this but bigger.
Put a cross on your outline wherever you have a joint.

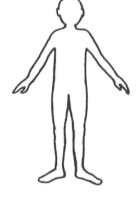

You can bend where there is a joint.

5. Think of some bendy movements to keep your joints supple.

Draw and write the instructions for a dance that uses these movements.

6. Draw a poster showing six activities you would enjoy.

Include:
  – two for suppleness
  – two for strength
  – two for stamina.

What do you do to keep active?

29

Coping with stress

These children have problems.
They worry about their problems, and they are unhappy.

Alex can never find peace and quiet to do his homework.

He gets into trouble at school.
Sometimes he doesn't go to school.

Hayley wishes her mum were not so busy.

Just a minute, Hayley. I'm busy.

Sometimes she is naughty just to get her mum's attention.
Her mum tells her off.

1. Talk to a partner about how Alex and Hayley might feel in each picture.
How does this make them behave?

Sometimes the way we deal with a problem can cause even more problems.

2. How does this happen to Alex and Hayley?

When people have problems they cannot solve, they sometimes feel stressed.

3. Discuss Alex's and Hayley's problems with your group. What could Alex and Hayley do?

Write letters to advise them.

Dear Alex
I think that you are going through a very hard time at the moment you m

Dear Hayley,
Things don't look very easy for you with your MUM being so busy with her work. Do you know why she is so busy at the moment? Maybe you could ask her
Good luck, Jo

4. Think of another problem that someone of your age might face.

Write about it on a postcard for a 'problem page' display.

5. In a group, discuss one of these problems.

Write a reply.

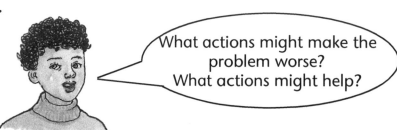

What actions might make the problem worse?
What actions might help?

Personal safety

Sometimes people we know and with whom we feel safe ask us to do things we do not want to do.

> It's so nice of you to come and see me, Rachel. You will come back tomorrow, won't you? And Wednesday and Thursday...?

> But Auntie June, I'm going to Jennie's birthday party.

> If you tell me what's the matter, I may be able to help.

> Rachel won't be coming today.

> She means no harm.

> But who else have I got for company?

Rachel has to go to Auntie June's house every day. But she wants to play with her friends.	One day she told her dad that she did not want to go to Auntie June's house.	Rachel's dad took Auntie June out to meet people. Family, friends and neighbours began to visit her.

 1. Draw the next picture for this story. Add speech bubbles and thought bubbles to the picture.

 2. What do adults ask children to do? Talk to a partner about what children should or should not do.

 Copy and complete the table.

> How did Rachel feel at the end of the story?

Things children are asked to do	Should they do this?

 Explain your answers.
How can another trusted adult help?

You are in charge of your body.
Sometimes it feels good to be touched.
Sometimes people touch you in a way or in
a place that you do not like.

I like it when
my nan gives
me a hug.

 **a**	 **b**	 **c**	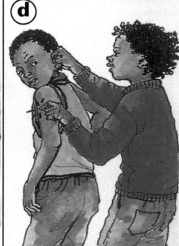 **d**
Ahmed does not like being tickled.	Pete does not like his big brother wrestling with him.	Ann does not like her mum's boyfriend to cuddle her.	Nick does not like his cousin pinching him.

3. How did each child feel?
Draw and write what you think
happened after each picture.

Copy and complete the table.

You are in charge
of your body.

Picture	What happened next
a	

4. What do you think each child can do
about what is happening?

What can you do if you are made to feel uncomfortable?

33

Influences

People know that smoking is bad for their health.

So what makes them start smoking?

① TOBACCO SERIOUSLY DAMAGES HEALTH

All cigarettes carry health warnings.

1. Which of the pictures, words or symbols might encourage children to start smoking?

   Which ones might discourage them from smoking? Copy and complete the table.

2. What other influences might encourage children to smoke? What else might put them off?

Explain your answers.

Picture	Reason
1	
2	

3. Why do many places have 'No Smoking' signs?

4. Find out about the effects of smoking:

Find out how smoking affects people's lungs and heart. What does it do to their skin and teeth?

The effects of smoking	
Harmful	**Unattractive**

Think about the smell of smoke.

Have a cigarette; it will make you feel good…

No thank you, not for me; I don't want nicotine in my blood.

5. Take turns with a partner to play the parts of 'persuader' and 'resister'.

Write what people might say to persuade and to resist persuasion.

Make your ideas into a play script.

HAVE A SMOKE – NO THANKS

Characters

Ringo Smoke (cigarette vendor)

Cool Sue (cigarette resister)

Scene 1: A supermarket

Nick O'Teen: Sue – I have just the thing to complete your image …

Relationships

1. How does Sara feel at the start of the story?

Why does she feel this way?

How might Zahid feel when he sends his invitations? How might he feel when he receives Sara's reply?

2. Talk to others about how Sara might feel when Gran tells her the news.

Why would she feel this way?

What other feelings might Sara have about moving?

<table>
<tr><td colspan="2" align="center">**Word bank**</td></tr>
<tr><td>afraid</td><td>sad</td></tr>
<tr><td>excited</td><td>scared</td></tr>
<tr><td>happy</td><td>settled</td></tr>
<tr><td>hopeful</td><td>sorry</td></tr>
<tr><td>miserable</td><td>upset</td></tr>
<tr><td>pleased</td><td>worried</td></tr>
</table>

high-rise flat

Gran

busy street

school

3. Describe how she might feel in three months' time.

Jack has just moved to a new town. He has left his friends.

4. What could Jack do to make new friends?

How could the children in his new school help?

How does moving house affect friendships?

Looking after friendship

When friends leave, you can still keep in touch.

1. In a group, decide what is good and what is not so good about each of these ways of keeping in touch.

Copy and complete the table.

You could think about cost, how often, time.

Method	Good	Not so good
email	Send message easily	Need a computer

 In what other ways can friends keep in touch?

Alice and Emily have been friends since they started school over 50 years ago.

Alice lives in Leicester now. She has two grown-up children and one grandson.

Emily lives in Cornwall. She has one child.

2. Write what Alice and Emily might have done to stay friends.

Some friends live far away and never meet. We call them penfriends. They write to each other.

3. Write a letter introducing yourself to a new penfriend.

4. How is this different from a letter to an old friend?

Ask your penfriend some questions.

There are other reasons for friends being separated. Talk about the reasons in your group.

How could you keep in touch with your friends?

Family fall-outs

1. Draw what happens next.
Include what Sam and his dad are saying.

Dad

Sam

Why do they say this?

 2. For each of these pictures, write down what kind of falling-out might happen next.

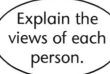  Explain the views of each person.

 3. Talk with a group about why the adult is saying 'NO'.

 Why is the child asking?

How could the child deal with this situation to avoid an argument?

What could the adult do to make the situation better?

Sometimes adults say 'No' or seem to be mean because they care.

Over what kinds of things do families fall out?

Stereotypes

1. Choose four people from the group in the picture.

What do you think each of them is like?

What do you think they like to do?

What made you decide this?

Talk to others to see whether you agree.

2. In a group, discuss whether you can tell what someone is really like just by looking at them.

3. Do the names in the picture influence what you think about each person?

In traditional story books, a grandmother often looks like this.

4. Think about grandmothers you know.

Do they match this stereotype?

What do you think grandmothers are like?

Carry out a class survey of grandmothers.

Think about age, appearance, interests, activities.

Discuss what you have found out.

5. Think about some other examples of ways in which we stereotype people.

How might people feel if they are judged in this way?

What about names, clothes, accents, possessions, where they live, school?

Do you ever judge people by their appearances?

Challenging stereotypes

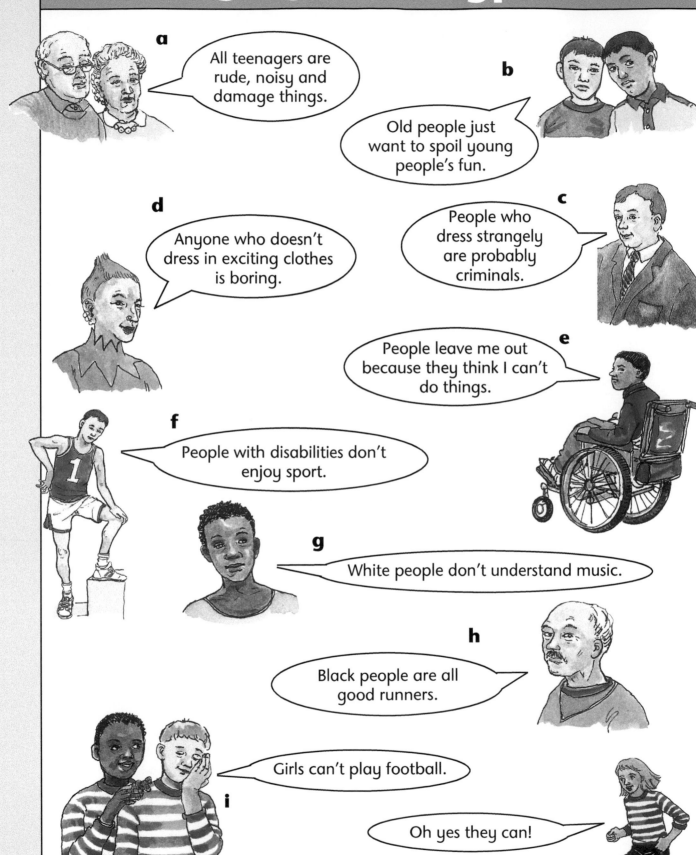

1. Think about each of the things being said in the pictures. Talk with a group about whether or not they are true.

Make a table.

True	False
a	
b	
c	

For each one, draw a speech bubble that challenges the stereotype.

Lots of teenagers are polite and care about others.

Some boys can't play football.

2. Draw two other ways in which we stereotype people. Add a speech bubble saying something about it.

People with red hair are bad-tempered.

 3. Write an answer to each one.

Why should hair colour have anything to do with temper?

People are all different. Hooray!

How can you challenge stereotypes?

Secrets

Secrets can be fun.

1. What was the secret in the story? Describe any secrets like this that you have kept.

2. Picture **a** shows a different kind of secret. How is it different?

3. Write a story to describe what is happening in picture **a**. Describe how all the children feel.

4. Complete these sentences.

An example of a good secret is _____ .

An example of a bad secret is _____ .

Sometimes people ask us to keep secrets that we think we should not keep or that make us feel unhappy.

5. What should you do about these secrets?
Discuss this with a partner.
Record your ideas.

Unhappy secrets

What we should do.

6. Finish the poem Can you keep a secret?
You could make it rhyme.
Redraft and illustrate your poem.

Can you keep a secret?

Can you keep a secret?
said the spider to the fly.
Well, that depends.
I want to know why.

Telling someone else can help us feel better about unwanted secrets.
Who could these children tell?

b) Make sure you have more tomorrow!

c) Don't tell anyone. I'm only having fun!

d) If I say so, you do it!
But I don't want to!

7. What should the children in the pictures do? Should they tell? Why?

b. The children should _____ because _____ .

c. The girl and boy watching should _____ because _____ .

d. The girl should _____ because _____ .

If you are asked to keep a secret, what will you think about?

47

Glossary

action (17)	Doing something.
alternative (11)	A different way of doing something, or a different idea.
antisocial behaviour (13)	Behaviour that hurts or upsets people.
bully (10)	A person who makes others do things by frightening or threatening them.
choices (14)	Possible things a person might decide to do.
consequence (11, 16)	Something that happens because of something else.
considerate (12)	Thinking of other people.
decision (14)	What a person decides to do.
destructive (13)	An action or behaviour that damages or destroys things.
disappointed (15, 21)	Not to have done what was expected, or been as good as someone hoped.
frightening (13)	Making people feel scared.
grateful (15)	Pleased, thankful.
influences (14, 43)	Things or people trying to make you behave in certain ways, make certain choices or believe certain things.
issue (10)	A problem that needs to be solved or talked about.
obtain (11)	To get.
offended (15)	To feel upset, or to have done something wrong or made someone angry.
opinion (11)	An idea or belief.
options (14)	**Choices**.
point of view (6)	What a person thinks.
relieved (15)	Pleased, not worried any more.
resources (18)	Things that can be used.
responsible (12)	In charge. Taking into account other people's feelings and needs.
rude (44)	To upset a person's feelings. To be bad-mannered.
senior citizen (10)	An older person (usually over 60 years old).
solution (11)	An answer to a problem.
source of information (11)	A place to find something out.
threatening (13)	Making people think or feel that they are going to be harmed.
vote (19)	To record your opinion or choice.